LOVE LETTERS
from an Ex-WIFE

*Confronting Hidden Feelings
that can Destroy Relationships*

KELLY D. SMITH

Dedication

This book is dedicated to my children for their love and patience in all my shortcomings.

"May the Lord bless you and keep you; the Lord make His face shine on you and be gracious to you; the Lord turn His face toward you and give you peace." **Numbers 6:24-26**

I love you forever!

Letters of Content

Acknowledgements

There are many people I want to thank for their perspectives, encouragement, support and love. First, thank you to my Heavenly Father "Daddy" for healing me and teaching me to receive Your love like I've never experienced before. My children, I love you both more than you'll ever know. I pray where I've fallen short as your mom that the love of God will more than make up the difference. My parents, all three of you, thank you for giving me the best of you. My tribe, thank you for your friendship, patience, support and love. It's priceless and you are family. Pastors Joel and Patricia Gregory, thank you for your wisdom, teachings and being a beautiful example of a Godly marriage. Bernard Williams, thank you for your counsel and wisdom that always challenges me to grow. Chuck Smith, thank you for your vision, insight, content and hours of editing you've spent pouring over this project. A special thanks to the Love Letters team. I am in awe at your support, encouragement, vision and wisdom guiding me through this project. Your teamwork made this possible.

Foreword

Three years ago, I had the fortune of meeting this woman who was all smiles and excited to be a part of our ministry here at Linked UP Church. As she joined our Worship Department and shared her talents and heart with our team, it was readily apparent that she had a story to tell and a reason for her passionate worship to God.

It has been an honor to mentor Kelly for the past several years: to pray with her as life has inevitably ebbed and flowed, to help her study and evaluate various books and study guides, and to see her grow into a true daughter of the Lord – a daughter that the world has been waiting to see revealed. (Romans 8:19)

I encourage every reader to walk into this process just as Kelly did, willing to risk losing the thing you probably hold dearest: the right to be right.

She has done the hard work of holding the woman in the mirror accountable according to God's heart and is sharing her lessons learned with the world. Her honesty and transparency have come at great cost and processing, but the harvest of her seeds sown will be immeasurable.

I know the Lord is proud of Kelly...I certainly am. And He and I are excited to see the "you" that will emerge on the other side of this powerful book.

Expecting Amazing,

Minister Bernard Williams
Worship Director, Linked UP Church

Introduction

There are many influences that have shaped the modern-day view of love, relationships and marriage. These influences have been reduced to a status symbol, a tool to be used selfishly, a vehicle for self-glorification, something to be used as a temporary fix or a great subject line for a hot new reality show.

The highs and lows of life come perfectly seasoned with beauty. The struggle can be recognizing the beauty even in the lows of life. While these lows can be challenging, we must remain mindful that the lows only prepare us to thrive in and appreciate the highs. True life success comes when we learn to balance life by remaining focused on constant love. There's nothing greater than love, it is the creative force, the only ingredient in the recipe of peace, the secret weapon against any foe. The only thing that can fortify love is finding a partner to do life with. Someone who shares your hopes and dreams, who encourages you, who supports you, who reminds you of your value, who challenges and motivates you. When you find a partner, who does these things for you and you can reciprocate, love and life bloom in unexpected and unimaginable ways.

Modern day pressures can cause relationship and marriage choices to be made out of hastiness, desperation, and emotion. This pressure can come from family, friends, or society at large and only contributes to unhealthy decisions where marriage is concerned.

The raw, transparent writings in this work explore important perspectives and questions that anyone must ask themselves before plunging headlong into a marriage. Be open, be honest, meditate on these letters. Ask yourself the tough questions, seek wise counsel, and make a sound decision about relationships and marriage. A decision rooted in confidence, knowledge, selflessness, and most importantly, love.

Author's Note

Confronting hurt and pain from our past is often something we avoid. Instead of avoiding it, know that there's a beautiful purpose in pain that can be transformed into peace and love. The pain we have experienced is often the pain we give out to others. Are you tired of hurting? Are you tired of the same relationship cycles?

This book is not for women only. Although these letters are written from an ex-wife's perspective, and in some places throughout the letters address women and marriage directly, it serves as a great guide for self-reflection, relationships, those who are considering marriage or already married. I intentionally chose a focus group that included men because I wanted to help ensure that this book would not come off as a women's only book. These letters may impact men and women equally by providing great insight and perspective to evaluate yourself and process past hurts that may impact any relationship whether with peers, family members, or within your social circles.

At the end of each letter is a section called reflection. This section of questions is intended to inspire thought, gain a different perspective and perhaps jump start your own journey to transformation.

"Make this your common practice: Confess your sins to each other and pray for each other so that you can live together whole and healed. The prayer of a person living right with God is something powerful to be reckoned with." **James 5:16 (The Message)**

Letter 1

Why am I Writing these Letters?

Dear Friend,

I'm compelled to write a collection of letters to you because I want to share the lessons I've learned about how I contributed to destroying my marriage by hiding my true feelings from my now ex-husband. During my healing journey, I became keenly aware of my part in the breakdown of my marriage and how I needed to own up to my responsibility in the hurt and pain I caused . I have also heard too many stories of men and women living unhealed and living out their pain in relationships expecting the other person to change. Listening to friends, I would say to myself, "I wish I had a platform to share what I've learned." So, this book is my platform.

Friend, please know that these letters are not for women only. In some places throughout the letters, I address women and marriage directly from an ex-wife's perspective, and sometimes I'm just sharing my feelings to you as a friend. Ultimately, I pray that they serve as a great guide for both men and women for self-reflection, those who are considering marriage or already married, and those who are divorced` and need time to heal before entering into a new relationship. *"Make this your common practice: Confess your sins to each other and pray for each other so that you can live together whole and healed. The prayer of a person living right with God is something powerful to be reckoned with."* James 5:16 (The Message)

I also thought about my children. As a parent, I have an assignment from God. Proverbs 22:6 in The Passion Translation says, *"Dedicate your children to God and point them in the way that they should go, and the values they've learned from you will be with them for life."* That has been my prayer for my children, despite my meager efforts as a young unhealed mother. (That's another book). My journey of healing has also been to pave the way to break family generational cycles for them so that they can know my mistakes and make better decisions.

Confronting hurt and pain from our past is often something we avoid. Instead of avoiding it, know that there's a beautiful purpose in pain that can be transformed into peace and love. The pain we have experienced is often the pain we give out to others. Are you tired of hurting? Are you tired of the same relationship cycles? I was!

So, here it is. I am not a pastor or a therapist. I'm just a woman that was tired of hurting and tired of hurting people. I was desperate for healing and intentional about going through my healing process knowing I would relive that pain. Each letter will be vulnerable and transparent.

I am calling these love letters because I don't have to know you to share a message of love with you. I contributed to the deterioration of my marriage by living out my pain, having toxic mindsets, not being a teammate, friend or nurturer. Pastor Isaac Curry says, "the pain we are often given is the pain we give out." How much of the pain in your past is being given out in your relationship with your spouse and others? I'll share more about that in another letter.

Does being in a marriage mean evolving? Absolutely! Does being married mean seeking the Lord for the needs of your spouse, family and children? Absolutely! Can this be uncomfortable and feel one-sided, you know, like you won't be loved back? Most definitely! God helped me to see that when I love my children the way they need to feel love, my heart is filled with joy when they reciprocate with gratitude and love. Philippians 2:3-4 in The Passion Translation says, *"So I'm asking you, my friends, that you be joined together in perfect unity – with one heart, one passion, and united in one love. Walk together with one harmonious purpose and you will fill my heart with unbounded joy. Be free from pride-filled opinions, for they will only harm your cherished unity. Don't allow self-promotion to hide in your hearts, but in authentic humility put others first and view others as more important than yourselves."* How much more should you do this for your spouse? When you ask God to teach you how to love the special people in your life, particularly your spouse, selfish motives are by-passed and new depths of love for them are reached. You connect with them and the love that lives deeply in them. Psalms 42:7-8 in The Passion Translation says, *"My deep need calls out to the deep kindness of your love. Your waterfall of weeping sent waves of sorrow over me like a thundering cataract. Yet all day long God's promises of love pour over me. Through the night I sing his songs, for my prayer to God has become my life."* You are God's physical and emotional expression on this earth to your spouse!

As I'm writing these letters to you, I have not yet had the opportunity to love a husband the way God is teaching me. Transparently, I am nervous but excited for my personal healing to be tested, for a chance to pour out my stored-up love, to be open to being loved, and to walk in purpose. I want to grow, evolve and to be challenged, but until then, I will continue to seek God, be intentional in believing Him for my continued healing and prepare for that beautiful day that is coming.

In sharing these letters, if all that is accomplished is for me to be released into greater healing, then that's its purpose and I'm good with that. However, I sincerely hope that in sharing, someone else can be enlightened, a marriage saved, or a union that isn't supposed to happen is avoided. My journey to self-awareness and healing has been through the lenses of biblical and spiritual truths combined with mental and emotional therapy. Kintsugi is the Japanese art of putting broken pottery pieces back together with gold – built on the idea that in embracing flaws and imperfection, you can create an even stronger, more beautiful piece of art. In my 14-year journey since my divorce, I've been beautifully broken. But if my journey is to share with you my pains, regrets, experiences, life lessons and wisdom of what I should have done differently, it is done so with the hope that it shares a different perspective, transforms your thoughts about your actions and brings healing to you.

Depending on your situation, it may be best to leave. No one can tell you when your enough is enough. If you are in an abusive relationship, please seek professional help. I've been in this situation too. (That's another book). However, if you have a relationship or marriage that's worth saving and is not abusive, I encourage you to please take these words to heart. In all, these letters focus on a journey of self-awareness, repentance, inner emotional and mental healing.

Friend, I need you to know that what I share with you in these letters was extremely difficult for me to write. No one purposely wants to put themselves at the risk of ridicule, judgement, embarrassment, and shame. For the most part, we all want to be seen in the best light and protect our reputation. To be honest, all of those thoughts crept in my mind, but it didn't stop me from my greater purpose - my desire to be obedient to God with this project for the promise of healing, breakthrough and freedom. I've carried this weight far too long and so I transparently share my life with you through God's love for me. Revelation 12:11 says in The Amplified Bible, *"And they overcame and conquered him because of the blood of the Lamb and because of the word of their testimony, for they did not love their life and renounce their faith even when faced with death."*

Love letters from an ex-wife,
Kelly

Letter 2

Are You in Love with Him or the Dream of being Married?

Dear Friend,

If you honestly asked yourself this question what would be the answer? Would you say, "Kelly, I dearly love the man I married (or about to marry). I'm truly in love with him." Or, is your answer, "I love him, but I'm not IN love with him." So, what's my answer? I loved my ex-husband, but I wasn't in love with him. I was IN love with the dream of the wedding and the idea of being married. I wanted the big wedding and all my friends, family and guests to pay attention to me. I loved wearing the dress and everything that came with that day.

If you were like me and in love with the idea of a wedding ceremony and the idea of being married, I can honestly say, you are not (were not) ready for marriage. I wasn't ready for marriage. My Pastors Joel and Patricia Gregory say, "Marriage is not what you can get out of it, it's how you can serve your spouse." If that's not your purpose, then you're not ready! See, I was ready for the wedding ceremony and all the pomp and circumstance. However, I wasn't prepared when the excitement wore off and serving my husband was the furthest thing from my mind.

We got home from our honeymoon and real life started the next day. Here's some of our story...

My childhood sweetheart and I began dating when I was 12 years old, he was 14. For the sake of privacy, I'll call him Mark. We met in our church youth group in Columbus, Ohio and dated for a few months, (which is a long time in preteen/teenage years). Even when we broke up, I was still infatuated with him. At 15, I moved to Atlanta, went away to college and moved back home to finish my last 2 years at Spelman College. While there, Mark and I began dating again, this time was more intentional. I was totally enamored by him, but I had a nagging question that plagued me along with a thousand other questions that swirled in my mind, "Why would he be interested in me? Why would he want to date me? Why does he want to be with me? What is it about me? Does he really want to marry me?"

You see, coming from a broken home (I am the daughter of a single parent and we lived with my grandmother) I had no example of how to be a friend to a husband, a partner, a helpmate, a teammate, let alone, a wife. To my detriment, I had a strict mental timeline: be married by 23-25 years of age, a list of the qualities of the man I wanted to marry, what I wanted him to look like, and how many children we would have by age 25-27. GEEZ! If you're not already doing it, let me shake my head at my younger self!

Preparing to get married was so exciting. Dress shopping with my mom, picking out colors, making wedding favors, doing the invitations and all the wedding stuff. One day my mom looked at me and asked, "I think you're in love with the idea of being married more than you are with Mark. What do you think?" In a blind arrogance, I blew her off. I even dismissed the teachings of premarital counseling. It wasn't until after my divorce that I realized she was right. I never took the time to examine if I was ready for marriage and what being a wife required. So, in 1996 at age 23, Mark and I got married. About 3 months before our wedding, upon my parent's suggestion, we took a week to pray separately about our future and if we should proceed with the wedding. I can't speak for him, but the first day I began to pray, God gave me my answer. Don't get married! I got the same answer every day after that during the week. When the week was over, we got together to talk about if we should still get married. I was so nervous to share with him what God told me. But my pride got the best of me. I began to think about my dress hanging in my closet, our friends and family that knew about the wedding and were planning to come and the rings we purchased. So, I said, "Yes, I feel like we are supposed to go ahead with the wedding." He agreed that he felt that way too.

As the wedding grew closer, we dreamed what life would be like married, but we never talked about the practical living "stuff". Like how we would pay bills as a new family. I remember when we sat down to pay our monthly expenses together for the first time that something wasn't right. We discovered in that moment, sitting at the kitchen table that we did not pay bills the same way. In 1996, there was no such thing as paying bills online. You could call the company and pay the bill over the phone, send in a check, or go to the location to pay the bill in person. Here was the rub. I liked to pay bills as soon as they arrived in the mail to avoid forgetting or any late fees. Then I'd send the check out in the mail the next day. Mark would wait until the bill was due. Then he'd send the check in the mail. Sometimes that meant paying a late fee. We completely disagreed on how to handle our finances and it was a constant frustration and argument throughout our marriage.

We also did not talk about how we liked to grocery shop. I remember the very first time we went grocery shopping after coming home from our honeymoon. Before we went to the store, I made a list but then there were other things that we wanted. We spent way too much money. By the time Mark and I got to the checkout line, we had two carts full of groceries. For some reason, we didn't put anything back. We spent over $300 on groceries, more on food we wanted versus what we needed.

We were married about nine and half years when things really started to surface. The truth of our marriage and who we both really were exploded like opening Pandora's box. During that time, things really started to unravel when Mark lost his job and the only employment he did find wasn't enough to pay the bills. When he needed me to be a teammate, I, metaphorically, slapped him in the face with my words and said to him what I had been taught as a child, "men are supposed to be the provider. You're supposed to take care of the family." I wasn't a teammate, and I wasn't his friend. I let people into our relationship by seeking advice from anyone and everyone rather than talking things out with him and seeking wisdom and counsel from our pastors or professionals.

Years later we revisited the prayer and fasting conversation before we got married and confessed, we both knew we shouldn't have gotten married. I told him I felt the pressure of how people would view us and the preparations we'd already made. He shared that he felt not getting married would be a complete break-up and a parting of ways if we didn't get married. Ultimately what he feared happened anyway, it was just delayed by 10 years.

I was extremely naïve in thinking that once I got married, I could just bring myself to the marriage and Mark had to adjust to me without me having to change...like it or not. After all, he's not going anywhere, right? Hmm, we'll talk about that later. I thought marriage was a coexistence rather than walking in purpose and always learning how to grow and evolve together. I was wrong.

Today I have a much different perspective on marriage. I have been intentional about unlearning what I thought a wife should be, reflecting on how I lived-out toxic actions in my marriage, taking responsibility for my part in the breakdown of my marriage, and learning what a Godly relationship between a man and a woman should be. I also know that I will need to remain flexible and open to my teachings to be tested and be willing to find solutions that work for both of us. I observed and am learning from those that make mistakes but are getting it right. They are examples to me from God what a true relationship looks like.

Even in our disobedience, God blessed us with two beautiful children, who bless me and teach me to be a better mother. I am so grateful for both of them every day.

As I shared earlier, I have not had the opportunity to put my new learning into practice. Being completely transparent, I know that my learning through my journey will be tested. Proverbs 27:17 in The Passion Translation says, *"It takes a grinding wheel to sharpen a blade, and so one person sharpens the character of another."* So, will there be clashing? Probably so. Will there be disagreements? Yes, there will be, but I'm learning through my current relationships how to be a friend, not one that leaks anger and hurt out on other people but someone who is not afraid to look inward to examine my heart. Remember, "the pain we're often given is the pain we give out." So, how do I need to change and grow so that I can respond in love and kindness rather than in anger and bitterness? In that same message, Pastor Curry also said, "You can't fake a healthy heart!" I hunger and thirst to be filled with more of God's love so that when the lessons from my journey come, when my husband comes, love pours out and not the pain of my past. It's my prayer to have a relationship with my new husband that glorifies God. Where I'm so in love with him that the ceremony is a time stamp on the day we committed to follow God and walk in purpose together.

Yours transparently,
Kelly

Reflection

Are you in love with your spouse or do you just love them?

_____

_____

_____

Are you in love with the idea of being married?

_____

_____

_____

Why?

_____

_____

_____

Are you in love with the dream of the wedding day?

_____

_____

_____

Why?

_____

_____

_____

Where did that dream come from?

_____

_____

_____

Letter 3

Are You Seeking God or Your Friends about Your Marriage?

Dear Friend,

I realize that I'm asking you another touchy question. The support of my friends and family is extremely important to me. I need my tribe and I value their wisdom. So, knowing this is a sensitive, touchy question, have you sought advice from your friends and family OVER asking God about your marriage? I have!

I was great at picking up the phone and venting. I would vent to anyone that would listen, including my mom. But what I really wanted was to be heard. I wanted my tribe to be on my side. I wanted validation that I was right. Somehow it gave me more confidence.

Let's say we'd be with friends and the subject of something I was venting about to a friend came up. I would expose the issue and vent to our friends in front of him to get our friends on my side in an attempt to force Mark to change or do what I wanted him to do. And not knowing any better, at the time, I also vented daily to my mom. Have you done this?

Listen, I'll be the first to tell you, I was extremely naive with little to no emotional maturity. I was desperate to talk to my friends, but I can also say even though they may have given me their perspective, that didn't mean I would listen. Let's be honest, sometimes our friends don't want to hurt our already hurt feelings.

As I reflect on that time, I ask myself, "why did I do that?" "What did I really need?" "Why did I feel I needed to get everyone's opinion and approval?" It goes back to my deep need to be heard from childhood, but also my insecurities of not knowing HOW to be a wife. Instead of venting about my issues with Mark, I should have sought healing and asked God how to be a wife to him. I knew the Bible and would quote Proverbs 31:10-18, but speaking scripture over myself and allowing scripture to transform my mind are two different things.

Friend, let me be clear, there's nothing wrong with asking for wisdom. Wisdom is described as having "attributes such as unbiased judgment,

compassion, experiential self-knowledge."
James 1:5 in The Passion Translation says, *"And if anyone longs to be wise, ask God for wisdom and he will give it! He won't see your lack of wisdom as an opportunity to scold you over your failures, but he will overwhelm your failures with his generous grace."* God gives us wisdom in many ways, so I do want to encourage you to please use discretion and foresight with whom you talk to. Not everyone is equipped to look past the issues to get to the root of your situation. A pastor, counselor or therapist are a few suggestions. Why did I suggest those people instead of my friends or family? Because they are usually unbiased in their judgement and compassionate towards your situation. More importantly, this will teach you how to create a safe space to protect your marriage.

I love wisdom! I love creating safe spaces in my relationships, I love getting to the root of my issues. I want to grow. I want a different perspective. I want to love more. I want to love deeper.

My friend, please, if you learn anything from me in this letter, protect your marriage and seek wisdom by asking God what to do.

Proverbs 9:11-12 in The Passion Translation says, *"Wisdom will extend your life, making every year more fruitful than the one before. So, it is to your advantage to be wise. But to ignore the counsel of wisdom is to invite trouble into your life."*

Always seeking wisdom,
Kelly

Reflection

Have you sought advice from your friends and family OVER asking God about your marriage?

_____

_____

_____

Why do you think you did that?

_____

_____

_____

Do you feel like you need approval?

_____

_____

_____

Why?

_____

_____

_____

Do you feel like you need people on your side?

_____

_____

_____

Why?

_____

_____

_____

Letter 4

He Chose You!

Dear Friend,

He chose you! When I say that, how does it make you feel? The 20 something-year-old me felt inadequate, unworthy, filled with a ton of questions and would shrink to the background. "He chose me" was a foreign thought to me even after Mark proposed. You see we had been talking about marriage for months and I knew it was coming, I just didn't know when, and I most certainly didn't understand the gravity of what it meant to be chosen.

We talked about marriage, looked at rings, set a date, and everything. I even went dress shopping and bought my dress before he formally proposed. In hindsight, man, did I put a lot of pressure on him! I remember during that time, he shared with me that he wanted to save money before we got married and get a roommate. I got mad, broke up with him and said that if he did that then he wasn't ready to get married! Whew! I'm irritated at my own behavior. How selfish...who does that? Me, I did!

One of the things that we liked to do was to go and listen to jazz at Hotel Nikko in Atlanta (it no longer exists), One day, he told me that our friends were coming to join us there for a night out. I watched the door waiting for them to come. That was part of the plan to distract me. Mark got down on one knee while we were dancing and proposed. It was a very sweet moment. Even though I had put tremendous pressure on him and was selfish, he still chose me.

Relationships are a choice, whether marriage or friendship. A joining of wills, of purpose, lifestyles, commonalities and differences. As I heal, I am unlearning old, toxic relationship mindsets that were running in my background like a virus hiding in the software on a computer, causing me to malfunction in my relationships. In recognizing that I needed to choose me for a while and be intentional about my emotional healing, I've experienced a greater love from God as He has gently peeled back the layers of my wounded heart to reveal what He wanted to heal. In turn, it's caused me to have a deeper awareness that He (God) chose me! Even in giving out pain to others in my pain...He chose me! Awareness brought tears. Repentance brought tears. Forgiveness brought tears. Praying for those that I hurt and that hurt me brought tears. Where there was once pain, anger, resentment and bitterness, tenderness, peace and love now abide.

I purpose that when I'm blessed with a husband, I will pray for him, treasure him, be intentional in my love for him and continually choose him. How will you be intentional about your choice?

Intentionally choosing,
Kelly

Reflection

Have you ever felt chosen by someone you love?

_____

_____

_____

How did/does that make you feel?

_____

_____

_____

Do you have feelings of insecurity or unworthiness in your relationships?

_____

_____

_____

What events in the past would cause you to feel this way?

_____

_____

_____

Letter 5

He Wants a Teammate

Dear Friend,

The generation you were born into can, and often does, influence your upbringing. Me? I'm Generation X raised by a mother of the "Silent Generation" and a grandmother from the "Greatest Generation." The Silent Generation children were expected to be seen and not heard, and the men typically worked while women stayed home to raise the children. The Greatest Generation children were raised during the depression and often grew up in poverty. They did things because it was the "right thing to do." Marriage was a commitment and divorce was not an option.

So, which generation raised you? Can you take an honest look at yourself and evaluate it against how you view relationships and how you think your marriage should be?

I remember as a young girl my mom telling me, "you need to find a man who's going to take care of you because men are providers." Yes, men are providers and protectors. That is their God-given DNA. But even as a young girl hearing my mom tell me that, I knew I didn't want to be a housewife. If you research each generation's view of relationships, it has evolved throughout time. I am a daughter of Generation X. We are the generation of independent latchkey kids that had to take care of ourselves because our parents worked, and are very independent, but also have the highest divorce rate.

As a Gen X'er in my 20's getting married, I was very capable of being gainfully employed. But my mom's words would play in my head like a skipping record, "men take care of women, men take care of women, men take care of women."

I got married six months after I graduated from college. I had a job as an assistant making $20,000 a year. In 1996 I thought I was doing something. Mark earned a little more than me. We started off living in a one-bedroom apartment when we got married. My job left me unfulfilled, and I wanted to quit., Mark and I talked and prayed about it. Mark agreed and I turned in my resignation. Two weeks later, I found my passion and began teaching private voice lessons which I did for nearly nine years and I loved it! I didn't earn nearly the money that I was making at my other job, but Mark discovered his passion in IT and got another job that earned more money. Teaching voice lessons to students after school in the evenings allowed me to be home with our children during the day until Mark got home in the evenings.

I like to think we were both content in our career paths for several years, but in 2006 life blew up! Mark lost his job and decided to change careers which led to a significant pay cut where ends did not meet. On top of that, that summer I got really sick and needed emergency stomach surgery. Scar tissue from previous surgeries tangled my intestines so it was pretty serious. Needless to say, I couldn't return to my teaching position at the school and this series of events allowed the erosion in our marriage to rear its ugly head. Being in the hospital for two weeks brought to light everything that we kept covered up for years.

Whenever things got hard Mark and I would remind each other, "We're on the same team. We wear the same jersey!" That was our code for teammates don't fight each other, we work together! At the time, Mark needed my help and asked me if I would get a job to help him. He didn't ask in anger, rather out of a true need for help. I remember I hesitated to answer him because at that moment I thought to myself, "what kind of job could I get that would make a difference financially? I'm not really qualified to make any kind of substantial contribution." All I'd done for 9 years was teach voice lessons, and I was burned out doing that. My insecurities and feelings of inadequacy overcame me and instead of sharing that with him, instead of being honest and transparent, I lashed out and said out loud what was playing in my head from my childhood, "No! Men are supposed to take care of the family," and walked away.

Friend, all Mark wanted at that moment, was a teammate. He wanted a teammate for the ten years we were together. As our lives changed throughout the years and we had children, I didn't change. We grew apart. More walls came up brick by brick that separated us, drove us apart instead of bringing us together as a team. We should have been constantly discovering each other and evolving.

Now in my late 40's, as I've said in other letters, I desire to be married again. I'm so excited to practice daily being a teammate, constantly seeking God for our marriage and praying for him. Trusting God to teach me how to be a helpmate so that he always feels like I've got his back. When he shares his calling, dreams or purpose with me, I will support him.

You are his teammate so purpose to be the supporter of his dreams, his best friend, lover, intercessor, defender of your safe space and his emotions! Remember, marriage is not what you can get out of it, it's how you can serve your spouse. Ecclesiastes 4:9-12 in The Message Bible says, *"It's better to have a partner than to go it alone. Share the work, share the wealth. And if one falls down, the other helps, but if there's no one to help, tough! Two in a bed warm each other. Alone, you shiver all night. By yourself you're unprotected. With a friend you can face the worst. Can you round up a third? A three-stranded rope isn't easily snapped."*

Wanting to be a teammate,
Kelly

Reflection

Which generation(s) raised you?

_____

_____

_____

How do you view relationships, and do you think your relationship should mirror how you were raised?

_____

_____

_____

How so?

_____

_____

_____

Does how you view relationships cause conflict in your current relationship?

_____

_____

_____

Why?

_____

_____

_____

Letter 6

Are You Asking God HOW to Pray for Him?

Dear Friend,

How does this question make you feel? It's not my intention to make you feel defensive if I did. The old Kelly would have gotten defensive and even angry. I would have said, "I don't need to ask God how to pray for him, I know how to pray for him." But I really didn't. Psalm 139:1-3 in The Passion Translation says, *"Lord, you know everything there is to know about me. You perceive every movement of my heart and soul, and you understand my every thought before it even enters my mind. You are so intimately aware of me, Lord. You read my heart like an open book and you know all the words I'm about to speak before I even start a sentence!"* Do you know your husband like that? No, that's God's job and that's why I asked if you are asking God how to pray for him. Especially when you've hit a rough place in your relationship. It's easy to ask God how to pray for him when things are great, but can you ask God how to pray for him when things are not so great.

When I was married to Mark, I didn't ask God how to pray for him. I thought knowing his Love Languages, his mannerisms and his likes and dislikes equipped me to pray for him. All those things are good, but they are tools used to get to know him. Knowing those things doesn't get to the root of his needs. Being his intercessor does! Romans 8:26 in The Passion Translation says, *"And in a similar way, the Holy Spirit takes hold of us in our human frailty to empower us in our weakness. For example, at times we don't even know how to pray, or know the best things to ask for. But the Holy Spirit rises up within us to super-intercede on our behalf, pleading to God with emotional sighs too deep for words."*

So, how has the new Kelly responded to this question? I've learned how to pray for Mark as his ex-wife. It was a hard lesson but one of the most beautiful lessons in my journey. He is not my husband, but he is the father of my children. That means he's family. Because I don't have interaction with him, I don't know what to pray for him, so I have to ask God how to pray according to His heart for Mark.

As I've said in other letters, I don't have a husband yet to test the lessons I'm learning but I'm looking forward to the day when I do. In the meantime, I have two young adult children that I ask God everyday how to pray for, and to teach me how to shepherd them in this new phase of life. There are many days I am at a loss for words on how to pray and even more days when I mess up as a mother. In humbling myself to ask God how to pray, He's given me more love in my heart towards my children.

Always asking how to pray,
Kelly

Reflection

How does this letter make you feel?

_____

_____

_____

_____

_____

_____

_____

Letter 7

Safe Space

Dear Friend,

Do you know what I mean by safe space? I like
how meetmindful.com describes a safe space.
It's where a person feels comfortable enough
to connect to the raw emotion of what is. Can
you make your husband feel safe? Absolutely!
In that safe space you are his sanctuary where
there's no judgement and no mocking. You
don't bring him pain or make him jealous. You
keep his secrets and respect him. And most
importantly, you don't criticize him. Does your
husband feel safe with you?

Well, I didn't know how to create a safe space
because I had unhealed areas that needed
validation and a voice. I breached those walls
by venting with friends and family. I was an
emotionally immature bride in love with the
dream of the wedding day. I was unprepared
for life after the wedding day with Mark. I
didn't know how to be a wife and I didn't

prepare for it. I had only prepared for the ceremony.

Occasionally, Mark and I would have fantastic intimate conversations where we would sit on the sofa and talk about whatever for hours. That feeling didn't last very long because I didn't know how to maintain that intimacy. I would be so excited about the conversation that I had to tell somebody about it later. Not all my safe space breaches were to vent. I'd never experienced the beauty of intimacy in a safe space because in that space are good things, not so good things, humor, irritants, making fun of each other, inside jokes, and so much more.

Sometimes when Mark and I would have a discussion, he could tell what I was saying was not my words. He would stop and ask, "have you been talking to "so and so"?" For a moment, imagine being in a room with your husband. You think it's just the two of you but there are cameras all around that room and what's being talked about is televised. Everyone watching has permission to comment about everything going on in that room. That's essentially what I was doing. When I shared or vented to the people I let in, I didn't know how to filter out what was sound advice versus what wasn't. I took to heart everything everyone told me. There's no way Mark could have ever felt safe or secure with me. You see, men need to feel emotionally protected as much as we do.

By nature, a man is wired to be protector and provider, especially with their wives. We as women need to understand that we must come alongside them as a teammate and protect too. Proverbs 31:11 in The Passion Translation says, *"Her husband has entrusted his heart to her, for she brings him the rich spoils of victory."* I want to say it again, men need to feel emotionally protected as much as we do!

Friend, please, learn from my mistakes to create a safe space in your relationship. If you don't have a husband yet, learn how to do it with your children or a friend. It will be good practice for when you do get married. I am!

Always a student,
Kelly

Reflection

What is a safe space in a relationship to you?

_____

_____

_____

Do you feel safe in your current relationship?

_____

_____

_____

Why or why not?

_____

_____

_____

Are you able to create a safe space in your current relationship?

_____

_____

_____

Why or why not?

_____

_____

_____

Letter 8

He Needs You to Listen to Him too

Dear Friend,

Have you ever said to your husband, "don't try to fix my problem, I just want you to listen?" I have. We all need to vent. But do you always say that and never want to hear his perspective? For a moment, put yourself in his position. How would that make you feel if that was said to you? I would feel like my perspective didn't matter. I'd feel shut down. Well, men can feel the same way. I want a different perspective and wisdom. I want someone to take my thoughts and turn them inside out to help me look at a situation differently. Some of my dearest guy friends are thinkers, introverts and observers. Men want to share their thoughts and feelings, and they want to be heard.

One year, I was on a business trip with Mark in Maui, but I was so stressed! We were dealing with some health challenges with our children, and I had mom-guilt for leaving them for a week. Our son was in occupational therapy for tactile issues with food, and our daughter had infant reflux. Figuring out what to feed them at each meal and for snacks was a daily challenge. Mark's work schedule was demanding, often requiring him to work long hours into the evening, often leaving me at home alone with the children. The work vacation was nice, but my thoughts were home with the children in Atlanta. Were they doing ok with my parents? Were they eating? Were they giving my parents a hard time with meals?

On that trip, Mark asked me a question that I'll never forget. Later, it played out to be the most pivotal moment of our marriage. He asked, "Are you still attracted to me?" For a split second, my thoughts measured my stress level and all that we were dealing with our children. Were these excuses? No, this is what was going on in our family that was affecting me. I didn't have the emotional maturity to communicate how I was feeling and instead of being transparent and having a mutual conversation of why we were both feeling the way we were, my fast mouth got in the way...again! I replied, "No, not right now!"

You see, growing up as an only child, conversation was not a part of my family culture, especially conversation that inspired or investigated thoughts and feelings. In fact, I was afraid to express myself at all for fear of getting in trouble for talking back or giving the impression that I was disobedient if I challenged a request. As a young adult, the mental and emotional insecurities from childhood grew with me and I learned how to hide behind my intelligence. So, when it came time to get married, I was missing the key component I needed that was sabotaging my relationship, honest communication.

Not only was I ill equipped to share my thoughts and feelings in a healthy way, but I also didn't know how to be quiet and listen to the thoughts and heart of a man or create a safe space where we could share without judgment, criticism and belittlement. Every so often we did have moments of intimate and transparent conversation. Those moments were so wonderful. I just didn't know how to maintain it. In those moments that mental software virus would pop-up and a wonderful moment would switch over to a conversation in my head. "Girl, don't just sit here and listen.

Say something to toughen him up. He's gotta get up and do something."

What I have learned over the last several years in my relationships with my guy friends is to learn how to listen beyond the words they are saying. God created them to be providers and protectors. But men are so much more than that. They have a tenderness that is only revealed in the safe space of your intimate relationship. They want to know that their feelings are being heard and being held with tenderness and care.

A few of my very dear guy friends are very masculine and strong, but every time I have a conversation with them, without them knowing, they teach me how to treasure their heart and value their vulnerability. They are all very different, but are Godly men with beautiful hearts full of love. No, they are not romantic relationships. God is using them as examples to me of healthy friendships. Maintaining that safe space with them is good practice for me when God graces me with my new best friend as a husband.

Always a student,
Kelly

Reflection

Men:
Do you feel you are not being listened to?

_____

_____

_____

What makes you feel this way?

_____

_____

_____

Women:
Have you said, "I don't want you to fix it"?

_____

_____

_____

If so, why do you say this?

_____

_____

_____

Letter 9

You're not always Right and that's ok!

Dear Friend,

Some women feel entitled to be right simply because they are women. Are you the type of woman that feels entitled to be right in a relationship, maybe because that's what you were taught by actions or examples? I know that's a touchy question, however that thought can be a societal expectation on wives. Where did that even come from? The saying, "happy wife, happy life" doesn't help matters either. I've even heard husbands say that they've learned to be quiet and just do what they're told. My perception is that way of thinking establishes a mindset of entitlement for women that is toxic. It breeds pride, selfishness and lack of humility. In turn, it can also breed anger and resentment in a man's heart.

I believe in a biblical family structure. Ephesians 5 gives instructions for Christians Households. The Passion Translation says, *"And out of your reverence for Christ be supportive of each other in love. For wives, this means being devoted to your husbands like you are tenderly devoted to our Lord, for the husband provides leadership for the wife, just as Christ provides leadership for his church, as the Savior and Reviver of the body."* That means that there is an unconditional love and sacrifice in his leadership." Later in the passage, it says, *"Husbands have the obligation of loving and caring for their wives the same way they love and care for their own bodies, for to love your wife is to love your own self."*

The Bible also shares how a wife should be to her husband in Proverbs 31:11-12. The Passion Translations says, *"Her husband has entrusted his heart to her, for she brings him the rich spoils of victory. All throughout her life she brings him what is good and not evil."* This was not me in my marriage. It was my mental perception but not the reality I was living out towards Mark.

I don't have a specific story to share because in every conversation, every argument, every negotiation I had to be right! And if there was push back, I would argue until I got my way, or there was a compromise where I got part of what I wanted. (Shaking my head at myself!)

Believe it or not, the Bible talks about a nagging wife. Proverbs 27:15-16 in The Passion Translations says, *"An endless drip, drip, drip, from a leaky faucet and the words of a cranky, nagging wife have the same effect. Can you stop the north wind from blowing or grasp a handful of oil? That's easier than to stop her from complaining."* Whoa!

All I can say is my mind and will have been transformed. I even have a disclaimer that I add, when appropriate, to my conversations. "I could be wrong, and I hope that I am but..." As I've shared before, I've lost friendships with girlfriends and more significantly, I lost Mark. So, why did I have such a driving need to be right? My need had nothing to do with Mark. It had everything to do with feeling like I didn't have a voice growing up. So, when I became old enough to speak up, right, wrong or indifferent, I fiercely fought to be heard no matter who I hurt. Sometimes to the point where I'd cry out of frustration. Mark was just the closest relationship to me, but he wasn't the cause of that pain.

Now, I have peace and God has healed that area in my life. I don't carry that burden anymore. I value the opinion of others, especially of those closest to me. I need their wisdom to grow and their perspective to challenge me and how I examine situations to make the best decision. As I've said before, I don't have a husband to test my transformation, but I look forward to it!

Gaining a new perspective,
Kelly

Reflection

Are you the type of person that feels entitled to be right in a relationship?

_____

_____

_____

Why do you feel this way?

_____

_____

_____

Were you taught this by actions or examples growing up?

_____

_____

_____

What can you do to change this behavior?

_____

_____

_____

Letter 10

Men hurt too!

Dear Friend,

Do you think that men are so tough that they don't hurt too? Why do you think that way? What was your example of a man growing up? Maybe you're like me. I didn't have a consistent fatherly example until I was almost 16 years old when my mom remarried. Two years later I left home for college so there wasn't much time to reshape my misinformed perceptions of men.

One of my perceptions was that men never get hurt emotionally. I'm a big football and basketball fan, and I have a great respect for our men and women that serve in the military. But in the same way we get physically injured serving in the military or playing sports, men get hurt emotionally as well. Men express feelings but will hide their emotions that's tied to that feeling. If a man cares anything about you, your words will hurt him.

One of the hard truths that I had to face in my healing after divorce was how badly I hurt Mark. Out of my own hurt, anger and growing resentment and bitterness, I hurt him with my words and actions. I watched him for years leave the house in the evening after dinner or after he'd bathe the kids to go back to work or go out with his friends. I was angry at him for always leaving me home alone with the children. At the time, anger, bitterness and resentment were building up towards him like a bank account accruing interest. I tried to be an understanding and complicit wife not realizing that I was becoming increasingly bitter over the years. Hebrews 12:14-15 in The Passion Translation says, *"In every relationship be swift to choose peace over competition, and run swiftly toward holiness, for those who are not holy will not see the Lord. Watch over each other to make sure that no one misses the revelation of God's grace. And make sure no one lives with a root of bitterness sprouting within them which will only cause trouble and poison the hearts of many."*

In October 2006, it was pretty apparent that our marriage was coming to an end. Mark and I took the children trick-or-treating and as we walked around the neighborhood, we were talking about our issues. He reminded me of our conversation several years ago in Maui when he asked me if I was still attracted to him. Apparently, my sharp, quick, insensitive answer in the moment made him feel unattractive and hurt him deeply. (His actions that followed are no excuse, but I can understand them now.) You see, my response provoked a desire in him to be loved and to feel attractive to someone else, sexually in particular. It finally dawned on me. I calmly turned to him and said, "I'm not enough for you." He said, "yes, you are." I disagreed and responded, "No, I'm not and I have to be OK with that." I wasn't trying to tell him how to feel, but I knew that he had needs sexually that I couldn't provide.

My hurt, my anger, my bitterness and my words chipped away causing an erosion of our marriage which resulted in an extramarital affair. It takes two people to create a marriage and both to destroy it. My part in this destruction was I did not value His feelings. I didn't listen to his heart beyond the words he was saying. At the time, I didn't realize that my words and actions mattered.

Words can tear down, add toxicity and destroy any relationship. The Bible is filled with wisdom on the power of your words. Proverbs 15:1 (ESV), *"A gentle answer turns away wrath, but a harsh word stirs up anger."* Proverbs 10: 19 (NLT), *"Too much talk leads to sin. Be sensible and keep your mouth shut."* Proverbs 12:18 (NIV), *"The words of the reckless pierce like swords, but the tongue of the wise brings healing."* Proverbs 13:3 (NASB), *"The one who guards his mouth preserves his life; the one who opens wide his lips comes to ruin."*

Just like our words can tear down, they can uplift, build up, encourage and be filled with love and peace, too! Proverbs 12:14 (NLT), *"Wise words bring many benefits."* Ephesians 4:29 (MSG), *"Watch the way you talk. Let nothing foul or dirty come out of your mouth. Say only what helps, each word is a gift."* Proverbs 18:21 (NIV), *"The tongue has the power of life and death, and those who love it will eat its fruit."* Proverbs 15:28 (NLT), *"The heart of the godly thinks carefully before speaking."* Proverbs 16:24 (NIV), *"Gracious words are a honeycomb, sweet to the soul and healing to the bones."* Proverbs 17:27 (NASB), *"He who restrains his words has knowledge, and he who has a cool spirit is a man of understanding."*

Mark is now my ex-husband. So please, trust me when I say I'm not judging you. My nature was to vent, lash out and respond to life as the victim. I shared with you how my behavior led to the downfall of my marriage. But can I share a different perspective? One of the many lessons I have learned in my journey is forgiveness. Ephesians 4:31-32 in The Message Bible says, *"Make a clean break with all cutting, backbiting, profane talk. Be gentle with one another, sensitive. Forgive one another as quickly and thoroughly as God in Christ forgave you."* Professionals define forgiveness as a "conscious, deliberate decision to release feelings of resentment or vengeance toward a person that harmed you, regardless of whether they actually deserve your forgiveness." Forgiveness frees you! We both had a part in the breakdown of our marriage, it wasn't all his fault, and it wasn't all my fault. I recognized my part in the breakdown throughout my marriage and then I forgave myself for my words and behavior that tore him down as a man rather than lifted him up.

Forgiveness is not a one-time action. Matthew 18:21-22 in The Message Bible shares a story about forgiveness. *"At that point, Peter got up the nerve to ask, 'Master, how many times do I forgive a brother or sister who hurts me? Seven?' Jesus replied, 'Seven! Hardly. Try seventy times seven."* Do the math! That's 490 times! I think what Jesus meant was that forgiveness is continual. It's taken me years to truly forgive myself and Mark, but I actively and intentionally practice and maintain forgiveness by praying for him regularly. Forgiveness freed me from the hurt we caused each other. Praying for him taught me to have a love that I will always have for the father of the beautiful children we share.

It's been 14 years since my divorce was final. It's been a long journey of healing and forgiveness, but I can honestly say that had it not been for the breakdown of our relationship and my divorce, I would not have learned these lessons I'm sharing with you or be the woman that I am today. So, rather than conform to your situation and respond to hurt in anger, what can you do to transform your thinking? Are you willing to have a different perspective? Can you take responsibility for your part? Can you forgive yourself? Can you forgive him?

Tearfully,
Kelly

Reflection

Do you think that men are so tough that they don't hurt too?

_____

_____

_____

Why do you think this way?

_____

_____

_____

What was your example of a man growing up?

_____

_____

_____

Letter 11

He doesn't have to Take it

Dear Friend,

Some people that believe that everyone needs to accept them for who they are no matter how they behave, talk to or treat other people. No changing required. Do you think this way? Have you ever said, "you just need to accept me for who I am?" The truth is, no, people don't have to accept you for who you are. Relationships are a choice. Behavior is a choice. Kindness is a choice. Love is a choice. But so is mistreatment, deceit and abuse.

Me and Mark's pre-marital counselors were our pastors and one of the things they taught was that you should be able to look at your spouse and say, "I want you, but I don't need you." Keeping in mind that relationships and love are a choice, here's the conundrum for me and that teaching. When you put those words in the mouth of an already hurt, angry and resentful person that is independent, it becomes a weapon that will wound the people closest to them rather than convey love.

So, one Sunday after church, I decided to test out that statement. I wanted to prove that I was an independent married woman. I looked into Mark's eyes and said, "I want you, but I don't need you." I could sense the cold callousness as if the words came from my heart and out of my lips like daggers. There was no love or gentleness in what I said to him. Belligerently, I just stood there, and I looked into his eyes thinking, did I really just say that? Yeah, I did and now he just has to take it and put it wherever he wants. Thinking back on that moment there was such pain and sadness in his eyes. I just dealt him another blow and chipped away at our marriage, again!

It's in our nature to be wanted, feel needed and to be chosen by the people we love. At that moment, I hurt him, and I didn't care. (Even as I'm writing these words, I'm in tears and am compelled to repent and ask God to forgive me for the hardness of my heart and the words I said that caused him pain.) About six years ago, I read a devotional called Enlarge: The Cycle is Broken by Vance K. Jackson. He references 1 Chronicles 4:10 (AMPC) that talks about how

"Jabez cried to the God of Israel, saying, Oh, that You would bless me and enlarge my border and that Your hand might be with me, and You would keep me from evil so it might not hurt me! And God granted his request." The Bible gives a brief highlight of Jabez, his name meaning sorrow or pain, describing him as a man more honorable than his brothers. You can sense his desperation as he asked God to shift the paradigm and change the trajectory of him and his family.

When I read this devotional, in tears, I cried out to God with the same prayer. I asked God to change the paradigm for me, my children and generations that would come after me. I realized that I had caused so many people pain from the anger, hurt, resentment and bitterness that lived in my heart. I carried that into my marriage and the other relationships that were around me. I was certain about one thing; I did not want to live that way anymore. In that painful existence, I lost my husband, friends and I felt like I was losing my children.

I don't remember Mark giving me verbal responses, but silence and actions spoke volumes. I believe that was his way of telling me that he didn't have to take what I said or how I treated him. When I came to an awareness of the pain I caused him and prayed that prayer, I've had a greater awareness of the power of my words. In my repentance, I pray for him. What I have experienced in praying for him is that God has put a love in my heart for him that I can't explain. It doesn't mean that we will be back together, as he is remarried, but as I shared in another letter, he will always be the father of my children and that makes him family.

Actively forgiving and loving,
Kelly

Reflection

Do you feel that your spouse is required to accept you for who you are?

_____

_____

_____

Why do you feel this way?

_____

_____

_____

Letter 12

Are You Taking Advantage of Him?

Dear Friend,

I know that sounds like an odd question, but are you taking advantage of him? Typically, women feel taken advantage of. But let's be honest, I mean really honest with ourselves. As women, we know how to take advantage of men, especially if we are emotionally unhealthy and in an unhealthy relationship. We've all heard the saying "happy wife, happy life." Are you using that saying to your advantage? Just to be clear, the explanation of what it means to take advantage of someone is "if someone takes advantage of you, they treat you unfairly for their own benefit, especially when you are trying to be kind or to help them."

In March 2001, our daughter was born. There were several complications during labor and delivery and as a result, I lost a lot of blood that landed me back in the hospital with pulmonary issues one week after delivery. The first time I nursed her in the hospital, she presented with infant reflux. After further testing, we came home with an Apnea monitor that would alarm us in case of a reflux episode or if she stopped breathing while sleeping. Nursing was a challenge for me because my diet was restricted to what she could tolerate, but she wasn't keeping her food down. I didn't suffer from postpartum depression, but I wasn't feeling my best emotionally or physically. I was heavier than I'd ever been and wasn't feeling attractive, not to mention, my body was not recovering well like it did after the birth of my son.

My daughter was born in March and that particular year Mother's Day was special because we had a new baby. Mark told me he wanted to go to Ohio to spend Mother's Day with his mom. I was immediately overwhelmed when he said that he wanted to go out of town, but I understood that he wanted to see his mom. I was upset that he was leaving me for a long weekend alone with the children with no help. I wasn't in the best shape to take care of them by myself. I just didn't feel like it was the best timing.

Watching tv one day, I saw a jewelry commercial for a Mother's Day ring; I got the brilliant idea that if he went to Ohio for Mother's Day then I wanted the ring as a gift. That wasn't really a compromise, but I took advantage of him to get the jewelry. The ring wasn't that expensive but at the time we had mounting medical bills and it wasn't a wise purchase. Our daughter's new treatment required specific medicine and care, and our son was in occupational therapy. By this time, we had been married several years, but I was still not a good communicator and wasn't honest with him about my feelings. Even if he still wanted to go, I should have at least shared how I felt. I didn't and I took advantage of the situation by asking him for jewelry.

For me, growing up as an only child, I didn't receive gifts from my mom out of guilt, but I was used to getting my way. So, in this situation with my husband, I wasn't getting my way, but I was going to get something! That behavior was embedded in everything I did.

Using my analogy again, in our formative years we can develop behavior that embeds itself in our operating system like a virus. When we try to behave in a new way or do something different the virus makes the new way malfunction. Mark wanted to provide for me but that did not give me the right to take advantage of his God-given nature. Can I challenge you to ask yourself a hard question? It's rhetorical so please dig deep and be honest. If this applies to you, where did that behavior come from? Why do you feel like you need to treat him that way for your benefit?

Ask God to reveal that virus, that hidden place in you so you can heal. Your husband deserves your peace, love and kindness, not your pain. Pastor Isaac Curry says, "past pain can make decisions for you." Is your past pain causing you to take advantage of your husband like mine caused me to take advantage of Mark? Does he really deserve to be wounded by your hurts?

Digging deep,
Kelly

Reflection

After reading this, are you taking advantage of him/her?

_____

_____

_____

Is your past pain causing you to take advantage of your spouse?

_____

_____

_____

Why do you think you do this?

_____

_____

_____

Does he/she really deserve to be wounded by your hurts?

_____

_____

_____

Letter 13

Don't Steal from Your Family

Dear Friend,

I can imagine you're thinking, "That's a weird statement! Why would you say that?" When I think of the word steal my mind immediately thinks about money, but I'm talking about robbing your family of yourself.

Let me explain. As individuals we are a part of a whole, in this case our family - mom, dad and children. In that unit, we have titles that have job descriptions. Mom and dad have defined their roles, but those roles vary depending on strengths and weaknesses. Maybe dad cooks because mom isn't so great in the kitchen, but she's great at cleaning. So, the teamwork still functions beautifully. Tasks change as children grow up and need to be taught responsibility.

In your role in your family, are you physically present, but emotionally unavailable? Do the wounds of past trauma cause you to build walls around yourself that keep you from connecting with your family? If so, you are stealing from your family when you are not emotionally present. Do work responsibilities keep you from spending time with your family? I think you get what I'm saying.

I'll raise my hand and be the first to tell you I stole from Mark emotionally for years. His love language was quality time. He was ALWAYS asking me to sit down on the sofa with him. In my mind, I had a thousand things to do, and they were my excuses! "I have to make the kid's lunches and clean the kitchen, finish folding the laundry, give the kids their baths, get them in bed by 8, and straighten up the house. I don't have time to sit!" You might be asking yourself, "can't Mark help with that list?" Yes, he did, but I was the scheduled taskmaster between the two of us. I always had a list and as a chronic busy-body, quality time was uncomfortable for me.

December 2006 was the last time we lived together. When I separated from Mark with the children, I had never lived on my own. I made an unpopular decision not to move in with my parents because I wanted to force myself to be present for everything. I didn't want to give myself permission to check-out! God blessed us with a home an hour away from my support system. Shouldering all the responsibilities as a single mother was heavy sometimes. I didn't always do great, but I did the best that I could with what I had, and God always provided for us.

Today, as I've been very intentional about my healing journey, I am even more vigilant about breaking the generational cycles that plague my family. I choose not to rob my children (now young adults) of me. I choose to be emotionally present in their lives while they both still live with me. The one regret I have is that I was not as physically and emotionally present for them in their younger years as I wanted to be. They deserved that. So, I choose to trust God with their lives, hope that they feel my love and pray that God redeems the time with them as He has healed my heart.

Choosing to stay present,
Kelly

Reflection

In your role in your family, are you physically present, but emotionally unavailable?

_____

_____

_____

Do work responsibilities keep you from spending time with your spouse?

_____

_____

_____

What steps can you take to make a change to be emotionally available?

_____

_____

_____

Do the wounds of past trauma cause you to
build walls around yourself that keep you from
connecting with your spouse?

_____

_____

_____

What are the wounds you need to heal from in
this area?

_____

_____

_____

Letter 14

Please, Keep Your Children Out of it!

Dear Friend,

When you and your husband argue, do your children hear the argument? Or, if you are separated or divorced, do you badmouth their father in front of them or to them? This is a really hard one because sometimes children hear more than we know. When we're angry and hurt, we usually don't care who hears us nor do we have much of a filter. And honestly, children sneak around to hear adult conversations.

In 2007 when Mark and I were going through our divorce, our children were five and seven. The county we lived in required parents to take a class called Parenting After Divorce and one of the things they said was that parents should never make their children feel like they have to choose who to love. When you badmouth the other parent to a child, in their mind, it's as if you are making them choose to love you. You're making them feel like they have to choose because of your anger. After I took that class, I immediately came home to my two children, looked them both in the eyes and I said. "I want you both to know you do not have to choose who to love. Just because mommy and daddy are not together anymore you can love us both." A relief came over them.

When we moved away, my daughter was angry because I made her feel like I was taking her away from her daddy. One day, I overheard her tell her brother, "I love daddy more than I love mommy." It hurt me to my core. Her statement stayed with me for years, but it drove me to make sure that I was not "that" mom that drove a wedge or perpetuated any kind of intentional action that separated my children from their dad. I never wanted them to feel that way, no matter my differences with Mark, I didn't want him to feel that way either. I wanted him to feel like he always had access to his children whenever he asked. Our children are now nineteen and twenty-one. In writing this letter, I asked them if I ever made them feel like they had to choose who to love. I also gave them the freedom to tell me the truth even if it hurt my feelings. They both said I never made them feel that way.

Honestly, I don't know that I've always done a great job keeping my emotions from them. I wrestle with my own feelings of inadequacy. Did I do my best with creating balance for them? Did I do the best I could with what I had? Do I teach them what they need to know to be great adults? Did I train them up in the ways of the Lord? 2 Corinthians 12:9-10 (NIV) says, *"But he said to me, 'My grace is sufficient for you, for my power is made perfect in weakness.' Therefore, I will boast all the more gladly about my weaknesses, so that Christ's power may rest on me. That is why, for Christ's sake, I delight in my weaknesses, in insults, in hardships, in persecutions, in difficulties. For when I am weak, then I am strong."*

My children are loved, and they love me and their dad!

They are my blessing,
Kelly

Reflection

When you and your spouse argue, do your children hear the argument?

_____

_____

_____

If you are separated or divorced, do you badmouth the other parent in front of them or to them?

_____

_____

_____

Why do you feel the need to do this?

_____

_____

Letter 15

What about Sex?

Dear Friend,

In letter after letter, I've shared about my part in the erosion of my marriage to Mark. So, I would be remissed if I wasn't open about our sex life. No matter your spiritual belief or if you feel like it's a taboo conversation, sex is a part of marriage, or at least it should be. Sex can give life to your marriage or be the death of it due to lack. I have a question that requires honest self-examination.

Do you withhold sex from your husband?

There are many excuses for withholding sex. You're tired, it's too late, you're too busy or just don't feel like it. Or, are you angry at him and hold out as a form of punishment, not just withholding for a day or two but maybe months? Do you find excuses to say no when he asks, but initiate sex when it's more convenient for you?

People have different levels of tolerance and persistence. Some people are relentless in their persistence and aren't going anywhere no matter what. Others, not so much. They've been told no one too many times and stop asking. Let's keep it real, they eventually stop asking and may go get the care they desire from someone else.

When we were married, quality time was Mark's primary love language. My primary love language is action of service. I wanted him to honor and respect my love language. In my youth and selfishness, I didn't reciprocate the same to him. I told him no much more than I told him yes. I had to fold laundry, do something for the kids, it was too late in the evening, or I was too tired. I think I had an excuse for everything.

I dealt blows of rejection to Mark' self-esteem by saying no all the time. I am not justifying his response to how I treated him by looking for love and affection from someone else. Again, I take responsibility in the breakdown of my marriage and I understand why he did what he did. I didn't do my part and I didn't do my part biblically as a wife. I own that. This passage of scripture is long but necessary. 1 Corinthians

7:2-5 in The Passion Translation says, *"...But because of the danger of immorality, each husband should have sexual intimacy with his wife and each wife her husband. A husband has the responsibility of meeting the sexual needs of his wife, and likewise a wife to her husband. Neither the husband nor the wife have exclusive rights to their own bodies, but those rights are to be surrendered to the other. So don't continue to refuse your spouse those rights, except perhaps by mutual agreement for a specified time so that you can both be devoted to prayer. And then you should resume your physical pleasure so that the Adversary cannot take advantage of you because of the desires of your body."*

Remember, you chose him, and he chose you. You made time for each other then, continue to make time now. Life and responsibilities will pull you away from time together, and by the way, it's ok to need your own time and space. One thing I've learned about myself on this journey is I value quality time - quality time alone AND with friends and family. It's much more important to me now than it was when I was younger.

Friend, choose him. Show him kindness, respect and love. Be honest and honor him and the relationship you've built, and humble yourself. In all of that, find new ways to experience each other so that you are always choosing him.

Won't say no anymore,
Kelly

Reflection

Do you withhold sex from your husband?

_____

_____

_____

What are some of the reasons/excuses you have for withholding sex from your spouse?

_____

_____

_____

Do you want or initiate sex when it's more convenient for you?

_____

_____

_____

If so, why?

_____

_____

_____

Letter 16

Please, Don't do THAT!

Dear Friend,

This letter is hard for me to write. But I wouldn't be able to write the entire book in this collection of letters without sharing this letter. So, what do I mean when I say, "Please, don't do THAT!" I mean, don't look for other people outside of your marriage to fulfill what you are not getting in your marriage. Men are not the only ones that have extra-marital relationships. The truth is women do it too. This is the ultimate breach of a safe space.

Yes, for a moment, you'll get a rush from the expectation of that call or text you get from them. And even more so when you lie to your spouse to make plans to see them. You'll get a high from how good you feel when you're with the other person especially when you've had sex with them. Those chemical rushes in your body and feelings you have are addictive like a drug. But can I tell you something? Luke 12:2-3 in The Passion Translation says, *"Everything hidden and covered up will soon be exposed. For the facade is falling down, and nothing will be kept secret for long. Whatever you have spoken in private will be public knowledge, and what you have whispered secretly behind closed doors will be broadcast far and wide for all to hear."*

I shared before that in 2006, I had to have emergency abdominal surgery to remove scar tissue that tangled my intestines. My health scare is significant because it was the pivotal moment in my marriage that exposed everything, especially our financial trouble and Mark's infidelity. I was in the hospital for nearly two weeks which meant he had to work and take care of the kids with help from family and friends. I can only assume that didn't leave much time for his other activities. (However, having been on the other side of that kind of a relationship as "the other woman," there is a feeling of obligation to keep them satisfied which can make you neglect family priorities).

Before my surgery, I began to suspect something may be going on, but I wasn't sure. When I got out of the hospital, recovery was very difficult which made it difficult to take care of the children alone. Mark had to work so my mom or friends would come over to me help during the day. They all told me stories that confirmed my suspicions. Rather than confronting Mark about what I had learned, I packed up some things for me and the kids and we left for my mom's house without telling him. When he discovered we weren't home, he called, but I refused to answer the phone. I believe eventually I texted him and told him where we were and why we left.

During that time, we were finally able to have SOME honest conversations about our relationship. Enough at least for me and the kids to go home. We decided to go to counseling. Obviously, that didn't work. For a few months, we lived two separate lives but were committed to making sure that the kids were taken care of. I was so hurt and angry, and out of spite, I chose infidelity as an escape. I thought, if he can do it, so can I! As I've said in other letters and will continue to say as a part of awareness, repentance and forgiveness, I own my part and take responsibility for every word that was not spoken in love or kindness. I was not a wife. I was a girlfriend posing as a wife. Every harsh word and hurtful action left deficits in Mark's emotional bank that added up throughout our marriage.

Pastor Isaac Curry said in one of his messages, "past pain can make decisions for you." It doesn't matter how far in the past that pain occurred. Yesterday, last week, last month, last year or in your childhood. What I discovered was when I became sober from the rush and high, the deceit caused me to experience more pain than I've ever known. Going through my divorce was painful enough. I hurt myself, Mark, my children and my family. I lost friends and experienced ridicule and shame that was almost unbearable. I had become someone I didn't recognize. I was lost. I knew God and believed in him, but I was so far away from him and everyone I knew and loved. The only way out of my situation was to turn my heart back to God by accepting my part through repentance.

I forgave myself and others and allowed God to heal me one layer at a time. I'm still on my way and as painful as things have been and as many tears as I've cried, I'm grateful for the journey. God has used the lessons to teach me what He needed to teach me to be where I am today and where I'm going tomorrow. That is part of the purpose of my pain. I believe I'm a better person, woman, friend, mom, coworker, daughter, niece, sister, girlfriend and one day, a better wife.

Tearful with hope,
Kelly

Reflection

Are you fulfilled in your marriage?

_____

_____

_____

Why or why not?

_____

_____

_____

Have you had a relationship outside of your marriage?

_____

_____

_____

If yes, why?

_____

_____

_____

Letter 17

Take Responsibility for your Part?

Dear Friend,

Are you able to recognize when you've hurt someone? Can you take responsibility for your part? When you hurt someone with your words or your actions, even if it's unintentional, are you able to apologize without adding an explanation that turns the situation back on them? An apology with a "but" is not an apology.

I decided to divorce Mark when I discovered he cheated on me with another woman. That was a hard pill to swallow because it attacked my self-esteem and thinking that I had done things right. I thought I was a good wife and mother to our children. I thought I was taking care of his needs. I blamed him for destroying our marriage and family. In my anger, I decided to do what he was doing. I cheated on him with another man. A couple of years after our divorce was final, I had to take a hard, honest look at myself and the actions I did that provoked him to go out and look for love, affection and companionship from someone else other than me.

I remember about eight months after we got married, Mark came to me at a very vulnerable moment and said, "I'm not the person you think I am." I had no idea what he meant by that and, honestly, I was too afraid to ask. I could only assume that he felt like he wasn't living according to the truth of who he was. I didn't probe and he didn't offer any explanation as to what he was dealing with. I just listened as he told me he was going away for the weekend to the Promise Keepers March with some men from our church. (Promise Keepers was an event for men in 1997 in Washington DC to mark a day of prayer, repentance and pledges to cleanse their personal lives, rededicate themselves to their families and work for racial reconciliation. The Christian version of the Million Man March). I was so confused. Fear and doubt gripped me. I was afraid to ask what he meant but I hoped he would find the answers he was looking for as he left for the march! All I could think about when he left was, who did I marry? How will I tell my parents that we're getting a divorce after only eight months of marriage? And what will he be like when he gets back?

When he came back from the march, he seemed renewed in his faith in God as he shared some of the highlights from the trip. We didn't spend a lot of time talking about it or rehashing the conversation we had before he left. I was too afraid to ask for fear of what he would say, and I just wanted to focus on how he was feeling in the moment.

In hindsight, I simply wasn't listening to him. I didn't listen to him throughout our whole dating relationship and marriage. I own that! So, friend, please be keenly aware that when a man is opening up and sharing his innermost thoughts, feelings and emotions, listen intently. Not just to his words, but his heart. Listen with love, kindness, encouragement, and most importantly, with God's heart for him.

Taking responsibility,
Kelly

Reflection

Are you able to recognize when you've hurt someone?

_____

_____

_____

Can you take responsibility for your part?

_____

_____

_____

When you hurt someone with your words or your actions, even if it's unintentional, are you able to apologize without adding an explanation that turns the situation back on them?

_____

_____

_____

Is this hard for you to do?

_____

_____

_____

Why?

_____

_____

_____

Letter 18

Do You Need to Heal?

Dear Friend,

I know this sounds like a personal and touchy question but really, do you need to heal? Do you need to heal from wounds in your childhood? Do you need to heal from a past relationship? Do you need to heal from hurts in your current marriage? Have you brought these hurts and wounds into your current relationship? Friend, if you answered yes to any of these questions, I promise you, the wounds will eventually leak out. Or, they will be exposed when something happens that triggers that hurt or trauma and makes you take it out on someone.

Why did I ask this question? Why is healing important? Have you ever been exercising or played a sport and you injured yourself? If you did, your physical body had to take time to heal before you could play or exercise again, right? I love to play golf. A couple of years ago I hit my elbow on the corner of the door and severely injured a tendon. Oh, I cried! My elbow hurt to the touch, shake hands, rest it on the arm rest of my car and to lift anything. When I finally went to the doctor, she told me that I had tennis elbow, not from use but from the injury. It took a year and a half before I could play golf again. When I finally decided to test my healing and play a round of golf, it felt fine. But towards the end of that summer, I was playing just a little too frequently and I stressed the injury.

Well, it's no different when you endure an emotional or a mental injury, you can't see it, but you feel it. Most of us are taught to toughen up and muscle through it. "Guys, man-up!" "Ladies, put your big girl panties on!" What if you can't man-up or put your big girl panties on because you're so emotionally wounded? I didn't realize how wounded I was and didn't take the time to look introspectively at why my relationships were failing. I didn't take time for myself to heal after Mark before moving onto the next relationship. Many of us skip around from relationship to relationship thinking that the next relationship will be better and end up getting hurt over and over again.

If you remember, I shared that I got married young. I was 23 and, in my mind, I was sweet, kind, pretty, intelligent and ready for marriage. I was a virgin when I got married and hadn't had any significant relationship heartaches from the guys I dated. My wounds weren't from guys but from the absence of my father growing up. I had deep festering wounds of feeling not provided for, unheard, unprotected, unnurtured, unloved, rejected and abandoned. When I got married, I expected Mark to fill this void. But friend, there is no person that can heal you or fill a void that only God can heal and fill. As a Christian, I believed God could heal my broken heart, but the information and teaching wasn't as available like it is now. As a 23-year-old in the 90's, mental health and emotional trauma were not talked about. Oh, and there was no such thing as going to a therapist. Like I said, I learned to push through pain and bury feelings, but feelings buried alive never die.

At the time that I'm writing this book, I've been divorced for 14 years. I've had several relationships come and go. In wanting a relationship so badly, I was piling on the pain one break-up at a time. When I finally decided to stop trying to have a relationship without being healed, I discovered a love from God that I've never known or experienced before. I discovered *"God's wonderful peace that transcends human understanding, will guard your heart and mind through Jesus Christ,"* like The Passion Translation describes in Philippians 4:7.

You see, if you don't deal with and heal from your wounds, they can have generational momentum. I've discovered that instead of running from my pain, there's purpose in my pain. It's not an easy question, but I asked God, "what am I supposed to learn from you in this pain, so I don't go back to it?" I'll share that in a later letter. When I made the decision to go through my healing journey and submit to the process, I made a decision to feel the pain all over again. The difference is that the people that hurt me were not there, God was. When I allowed God to lead me through my journey, the pain I felt was in a safe space covered by His love. When I was in my safe space with God, it compelled me to be honest with myself and ask myself hard questions about why I felt the way I did. I cried a lot, sometimes I was angry, but I allowed myself to feel all of those feelings in the moment. I didn't push any feelings away.

Remember, you can't fake an emotionally healthy heart because the pain we're often given is the pain we give out. Dr. Caroline Leaf says, "the hard and uncomfortable truth is that sometimes healing requires you to take an honest and critical (but compassionate) assessment of the role you played in the struggle and your suffering." My beautiful friend, please be willing to take the journey through healing so that you don't take your wounded heart into meaningful relationships. When I reflect on my life prior to my journey, I used to feel such shame over the friends I hurt and lost, the pain I caused my family, and that it cost me my marriage. Today, I am a better woman, friend, daughter, and mother.

Healing,
Kelly

Reflection

Can you recognize some wounds from your childhood?

_____

_____

_____

What are some of those wounds?

_____

_____

_____

Do you need to heal from past relationships?

_____

_____

_____

What are some of the wounds?

_____

_____

_____

Do you need to heal from hurts in your current marriage?

_____

_____

_____

Have you brought these hurts and wounds into your current relationship?

_____

_____

_____

Are you willing to take the journey to heal from these hurts and wounds?

Letter 19

Can You Pray for Your Ex-husband?

Dear Friend,

I pray you never get to this place in your relationship. But, if you do, I can only imagine what you're saying! Why would I do that? I know, it was an impossible thought for me too. Now, I'm not talking about the kind of prayer where you complain to God about what he did to you. No, I'm talking about the kind of prayer you probably don't want to pray. Matthew 5:43-44 in The Passion Translation says, *"Your ancestors have also been taught 'Love your neighbors and hate the one who hates you.' However, I say to you, love your enemy, bless the one who curses you, do something wonderful for the one who hates you, and respond to the very ones who persecute you by praying for them."*

I can hear you now, "Kelly, really? I can't do that! What's in it for me?" It will free you from anger, bitterness and resentment which ties your emotions to them. It also changes your

heart to walk in forgiveness towards them.
Remember what I said in an earlier letter,
forgiveness is not a one-time action. Jesus said
forgive seventy times seven! AND forgiveness
must be maintained by continually praying for
them. It's too easy to slip back into
unforgiveness if you don't.

Since our divorce, I've observed from a distance
that Mark has gone through a lot of pain. My
heart goes out to him. I can't take all of his pain
away, but I can apologize for the pain I caused
him years ago. I may not be his wife anymore,
but he is still family to me because he is the
father of our two beautiful children. And
because he is their father, I pray for him
earnestly that God would heal him, that God
would pour out His love for him and that he
would feel it in the way that only God can
customize that feeling for him. I'm not in love
with him but I have a love for him that only God
could give me.

Maintaining forgiveness,
Kelly

Reflection

Are you divorced?

_____

_____

_____

Do you have an awareness of your actions that played a part that led to divorce?

_____

_____

_____

How do you feel about that?

_____

_____

_____

Letter 20

Encouragement

Dear Friend,

Since this is my last letter and the other letters were pretty heavy, I want to make sure you feel encouraged. Please understand that as I have taken responsibility and acknowledge my part in my failed marriage, I fully understand that it is not all my fault. But it's not all Mark's fault either. For years I blamed him as if I had nothing to do with our failed marriage. I was wounded and hurt. I lived out my pain onto Mark. Our failed marriage was not all my fault, but it is my responsibility to heal.

Psalm 32:1-7 in The Passion Translation says, *"What bliss belongs to the one whose rebellion has been forgiven, those whose sins are covered by blood. What bliss belongs to those who have confessed their corruption to God! For he wipes their slates clean and removes hypocrisy from their hearts. Before I confessed my sins, I kept it all inside; my dishonesty devastated my inner life, causing my life to be filled with frustration, irrepressible anguish, and misery. The pain never let up, for your hand of conviction was heavy on my heart. My strength was sapped, my inner life dried up like a spiritual drought within my soul. Then I finally admitted to you all my sins, refusing to hide them any longer. I said, "My life-giving God, I will openly acknowledge my evil actions." And you forgave me! All at once the guilt of my sin washed away and all my pain disappeared! This is what I've learned through it all: All believers should confess their sins to God; do it every time God has uncovered you in the time of exposing. For if you do this, when sudden storms of life overwhelm, you'll be kept safe. Lord, you are my secret hiding place, protecting me from these troubles, surrounding me with songs of gladness! Your joyous shouts of rescue release my breakthrough."*

As a part of my healing journey, I prayed a lot. I listened to hours of sermons on healing and relationships from my Pastors Joel and Patricia Gregory and Pastor Jerry Flowers. I used mental health techniques from Dr. Caroline Leaf, a Neuroscientist, mental health and mind expert. She says, "There is nothing wrong with you. You just have patterns to unlearn and wounds to heal. There is nothing wrong with the core of who you are."

Are you tired of hurting? Are you tired of the same relationship cycles? I want to encourage you to take the first step and acknowledge your pain and areas of hurt for God to heal them, so you'll never return to them. But you've got to be intentional and put in the effort. Meg Sylvester said, "Expecting things to change without putting in any effort is like waiting for a ship at the airport."

Are you ready to heal and be whole? And just so we're clear, healing means to become healthy again - whole means to become complete and unbroken! Isaiah 38:16-17 in The Message Bible says, *"O Master, these are the conditions in which people live, and yes, in these very conditions my spirit is still alive - fully recovered with a fresh infusion of life! It seems it was good for me to go through all those troubles. Throughout them all you held tight to my lifeline. You never let me tumble over the edge into nothing. But my sins you let go of, threw over your shoulder - good riddance!"*

Choosing to heal is choosing to feel the pain all over again. As Pastor Jerry Flowers says, "there is pain in recovery." It hurts to break a leg, but it also hurts to get that leg set by the doctor so it can heal properly. Then the doctor prescribes pain medication after you get the cast on until the pain subsides. And while the bone is healing, your leg is in the cast for weeks, insulated from outside elements to protect it from becoming hurt during the healing process. Such is the emotional healing process when you allow your Heavenly Father to "set" the broken places and insulate you as He guides you through your process in love and tenderness.

1 Corinthians 13:4-8 in The Passion Translation says, *"Love is large and incredibly patient. Love is gentle and consistently kind to all. It refuses to be jealous when blessing comes to someone else. Love does not brag about one's achievements nor inflate its own importance. Love does not traffic in shame and disrespect, nor selfishly seek its own honor. Love is not easily irritated or quick to take offense. Love joyfully celebrates honesty and finds no delight in what is wrong. Love is a safe place of shelter, for it never stops believing the best for others. Love never takes failure as defeat, for it never gives up. LOVE NEVER STOPS LOVING."*

I've often read this passage as how I'm supposed to love others. But have you ever read it as a love letter from God to you? Read it again with that in mind.

Because Jesus loves me, I choose to receive His love for me and to love others. Friend, I'll end my letter with a simple confession I heard from Pastor Jerry Flowers. From this day forward, "you will no longer know me by my wounds! I am healing, healed and whole in Jesus name!"

Peace and Love,
Kelly

Reflection

Are you tired of the same relationship cycles?

_____

_____

_____

Are you tired of hurting?

_____

_____

_____

Do you feel like you are ready for your own healing journey?

_____

_____

_____

Write your own love letter!

Here's a letter template as a tool to begin your own healing journey. You can get your thoughts out or give to someone. Either way, writing the letter will be liberating.

Dear _____,

_____

_____

_____

_____

_____

_____

_____

_____

_____

_____

_____

_____

_____

_____

_____

_____

_____

_____

_____

_____

_____,

_____

(Your name)

Let's Connect!

Love Letters on Purpose

loveletters.onpurpose

KellyOnPurpose.com

Made in the USA
Columbia, SC
27 June 2021